How To Get And Keep The Best Jobs

A. Donenfeld

DEDICATION

To the dedicated people who energized my offices for
more than 40 years with their vitality and strength, charm
and compassion, diligence and patience, elegance and
grace—I give you my unending thanks and appreciation.
Successes would have been empty and defeats crushing
without you. You made coming to work every day a joy.

And to all those recent graduates who need a
little hand holding as they trek through the morass of
trying to find a decent job in a poor economy, I've
provided some tips to hold on to.

CONTENTS

Contents

Introduction

Just graduating from school? Have you been hearing about the job market and how difficult it is to get a job, any job, not just the one you've been hoping for? There are plenty of books on the market that give you ideas how to get a job, but most of them are written by people who have never had the best jobs in the world, or hired people to work for them.

I've had the world's best jobs and have hired people to work for me so I know, from both sides of the desk, how to empower you to find, get and keep the best jobs in the world.

I'm Alice Donenfeld, a New York City attorney who started out representing major Broadway producers like Richard Rogers and Hal Prince, going on to become Vice President of Marvel Entertainment where my clients were the likes of Spiderman, The Incredible Hulk and Captain America. I then went to Filmation Studios, a large animation studio, as Executive Vice President where I spent years globetrotting at world television conventions with He-Man and the Masters of the Universe, She-Ra Princess of Power and Fat Albert. I've consulted with companies as diverse as DIC Entertainment (Inspector Gadget, Sonic the Hedgehog, Madeline) and Bavaria Film Studios GmbH, Faith and Values Media and many others.

For eighteen years I had my own company where I produced and sold over 100 episodes for television, and distributed thousands more episodes of television programs to broadcasters world-wide. I taught "The Business of Television in a Digital World" at UCLA and have been an entertainment industry speaker for over 30 years.

I hired and trained my staffs for many decades and can share my secrets of what I looked for in new recruits.

When I went for my first professional job as a lawyer, I had a long resume with jobs that ranged from chauffeur to hat check girl in night clubs. I had worked my way through both college and law school. A prospective employer wouldn't have seen experience in my new profession, but they would see I had been determined to succeed and wouldn't let a little thing like the need to earn a living deter me from my dream. That kind of ambition and determination counts for a lot.

I will tell you not only what I looked for in first impressions, but also how to behave in interviews, how to do an eye-catching resume, the do's and don'ts in interview protocol, and how to find the perfect job for you.

But that's only half the story. The other half is how to keep the job once you have it. There are times when a new employee looks great at the interview, but doesn't live up to their first impression. This book has eight secrets of how to keep the best jobs and how to move up the ladder to success.

Let's get started right now, the ladder to success starts with the first step up!

Chapter 1. The Best Job For <u>You?</u>

You have just graduated and now is the time to get started on the journey towards a lifetime career. It seems like there isn't much to it, just find someone who will hire you. Stop! Right there! Let's give this decision some thought. There are a lot of factors that go into making this serious kind of decision. Let's make a list to figure it out.

1. What do you like to do best? Make a

list and write it below

_____

_____

_____

2. What are your skills?

    _____

    _____

3. What are you good at *and* like to

    do?_____

    _____

4. What is your favorite hobby?

    _____

    _____

5. What is your favorite sport?

    _____

    _____

6. What did your education equip you

    to do?

    _____

    _____

That gives you a profile of your skills,

education and what you find interesting.
Next, where do you want to live and work?

_____

_____

If this is where you now live, figure out how
much it will costs you to live there. If you are
living with your parents, the number should be
how much you will contribute for your share of
the family living expenses. Every good
business person knows they have to share
their part of the costs, start now.
In your calculation, you have to include:

    1. Rent per

       month_____

    2. Utilities_____

    3. Food_____

    4. Insurance_____

    5. Commuting (auto, gas, bus, train,

       parking, etc.) per month

       _____

       _____

What companies produce products or do the

kind of work that you like best? This can be video games, sports equipment, entertainment, restaurants or chains, retail businesses, farm equipment, music, research, medical – whatever your interest is. List them below, try to think of ten or more.

_____

_____

_____

_____

_____

_____

Where are these companies located? Are any of them within thirty minutes commute of where you live? If so, these are the first places to target as prospective employers.

The next step is to Google all of the companies on your target list, read their annual reports, check out their web sites, read all the press releases, see if they have a Human Resources area on their web site with job postings. When you have read all the information, make sure you are aware of what their financial situation is – are they hiring or firing employees? Is the company growing or downsizing? This information is important for your future. Also, if you get your foot in the door for an interview, you will be knowledgeable in speaking about the company.

If the company is listed on the stock market you can easily research them on-line by going to a brokerage service like Charles Schwab or e-trade and looking at the last six-months financials and press releases.

If there are no companies within commuting distance of where you now live, then you have to calculate the cost of moving to another location, or, go to your next favorite thing to do and repeat the process of finding what companies are within a reasonable distance.

If you are married, all these variables should be discussed in detail with your spouse. Both of you need to agree on location, cost of living, and all the other parameters of a new career. How much time will you be away from home? Will you have to work long hours? Have a long commute? Work nights? Work weekends? Will you be taking a permanent job, or just working on a short term contract? Your spouse must be aware of all these decisions because you will need their agreement to be the best employee possible. No one can do a good job when an angry spouse is on the telephone constantly complaining or showing up annoyed at the workplace. You might be taking the job, but your spouse has to be a partner in the decision.

Perhaps you might take a lower paying position to get in on the ground floor where the future might hold better prospects than a higher paying job with a dead end. It might entail a spouse working as well with two incomes necessary at first to maintain your cost of living. There can be no secrets at this juncture because there are two futures at stake.

Considering marriage? Consider the impact the future Mr. or Mrs. might make on your career. Will they be a good partner for you at business functions? It might seem farfetched to think about but a badly behaved partner can be a detriment at business events and can cause employers to question your sound judgment. A helpful partner who makes a good impression can be an excellent asset on the ladder to success

Chapter 2: 5 Reasons Why A First Job Can Be Your Most Important

Think of a large well-fortified castle and you are a knight wanting to get inside to the Princess, your true love. The gatekeeper of that castle is the Human Resources Department ("HR") and they man the drawbridge you have to cross just to get to the first gate.

HR is presented with lists of approved job openings by each department within the company and their job is to find candidates who fit the job descriptions. They present the candidates to the department heads and prospective supervisors/bosses who review the resumes and decide which of the candidates are interesting enough to go to the next step – first interview with HR. If they are acceptable to HR, they will be interviewed by the department heads or supervisors where they will eventually work.

HR looks for certain things. Most companies have a policy of non-discrimination in hiring. This is in compliance with government regulations. Minorities that are not already represented in the company may have an advantage if they are skilled.

They will look at appearance to see if the candidate will be a good fit with the company. Attitude, hygiene, education, flexibility and sincerity all play a part in the selection. A high maintenance candidate with a lot of demands or an attitude problem is not a good candidate. Apply for any position posted by HR that you could possibly do **even if you think it is below your skill set.**

Take any job in the company of your choice – most companies like to promote and hire for new positions from within. This gives you a front row seat ahead of outside applicants when better jobs become available!

Make friends with the HR Department

personnel if you can. Make sure they know your skills and that you want to stay with the company and move into other positions if they become available. This also makes their life easier if they have a ready and willing candidate for a new opening. Especially since it will be easy for them to check on how you have been doing in your previous position.

If you are moving to a different location, the suggestions change a bit. Remember in Chapter 1 where you made a calculation of your living expenses? Well, you need this information to assess how low-paying a start-up job you can take as you will have living expenses to take care of. You have to include taxes as part of your expenses and find out what your "take home pay" will be after deductions for taxes and perhaps medical insurance as well as FICA. You might end up with little extra money to spend during the course of this first job, but consider it an investment in your future.

The first job in your chosen profession or business is very important for five very important reasons:

I. It will give you something to put on your resume

II. It is always easier to get a job if you already have one

III. It shows you are trying to learn a particular business from the ground up – always a prime indication of seriousness

IV. If you do a good job and have a good report with your boss or supervisor, it means a good reference when taking the next step up, whether in the same company to a different position, or with another company

V. If there is a nearby competitor in the same industry, they will likely be interested in you after you gain some experience in how someone else does the job

Chapter 3: Prepare Your Resume

The most important thing to remember is that there is only one chance to make a good first impression! Your resume is that chance. If that gets you in the door, your interview is the second chance. Make them both the best you can.

Start your resume with one sentence of your goal, not more than twenty words, and in it make sure you tell the company what you can do for them.

Most people starting out don't have too much information to put in a resume, so put in your education... AND DON'T LIE ABOUT IT! This is one of the most common mistakes and it is a fatal error. If HR checks and finds that you haven't told the truth, you are forever out that door.

Many people feel they have to exaggerate their education or job history to get in the door. This is akin to a kiss of death if HR checks up on you…and they do many times. It is better to have a thin and accurate resume than an impressive and exaggerated one.

It can be as simple as:
2010 ABC College BA in Creative Writing *(list most current first with major)*
2006 XYZ High School – College preparatory
College Activities: Debating Society, Theatre Club
Sports: Rowing team *(these things show you are interested in more than just getting an education, can show also that you are a team player)*
Awards: list if any
Languages: *(if you speak another language it's a big plus)*
Memberships: list if any
Job History: list if any, most current first, include dates worked and position held, even summer or part time jobs help, they show you

are willing to work
Make sure the resume is clean, clear, well punctuated, correct grammar and spelling. If you have a bare bones resume, you can include letters of reference from clergy or school such as "good worker, willing to volunteer for school activities" or "always helped with church fund raising events." These show that you are helpful and not afraid of a little extra work, always a plus if the resume is otherwise thin.

Some common mistakes are making resumes too dense, too wordy. Most people want to pick up a resume and see education, experience, skills and references. If there are a lot of extraneous materials, it might be put in the "no" pile for the simple reason that no one wants to take the time to read it.

> *A resume is the first impression you give to a prospective employer. Make sure it's a good one.*

> *Number one priority on the*
> *list of anyone in a capacity to*
> *hire will be to make sure a*
> *new employee will not lose*
> *the company any clients.*

Chapter 4: Let's Talk Entitlement

The truth of the matter is, no one in this day and age is entitled to anything. I'm going to talk to you like your parents probably never had, so listen carefully, this is information that will take you from flipping burgers to a good job.

Finding a good job is the hardest job you might ever have. Yes, I mean what I said, finding a job is a job. The unemployment rate today among high school graduates and college graduates is the highest it has ever been since the 1930's.

You are *not* special. There are hundreds, perhaps thousands, of candidates with the same skill set and as smart if not smarter than you are. All of them are as entitled as you are to get a job. Most of them have not read this book. That puts you one step ahead of them all.

Here are all the things that would make me *not* hire you on sight when you first walk in the door. If you have them, loose or hide them:

Sloppy appearance.

Dirty fingernails.

Dirty clothes.

Tangled hair.

Dirty shoes.

Bitten nails and torn cuticles.

Butt crack.

Bare midriff.

Ear gages.

Arms filled with tattoos.

Piercings, especially tongue piercing.

Bright un-natural colored hair.

Odd hairstyles.

Using the word "like' constantly.

Using texting slang in written pieces.

Slouching.

Scratching crotch.

Jeans with holes unless you are doing manual

labor.
Overtly sexual behavior.
Overtly flamboyant sexuality.
Overt display of religious symbolism.

Human resources cannot tell you any of this as it is against company policy. You have asked me by buying this book. I can tell you the truth. Now I'll tell you the 'why?'

First, because I don't want to look every day at someone who annoys me.
Second, because I don't want my clients or people I do business with to be subjected to people with the above, and that is because:
Something in the list might be offensive to their religion.
Something in the list they might find personally offensive.
Something in the list might be distasteful to them.

This is business.

There is no way I will pay someone who might offend a client and cause me to lose business. That will be number one on the list of anyone in a capacity to hire. When I was hiring people for international sales positions I noted if they wore large religious symbols, crosses, star of David. If so, they were not considered. Religious discrimination? Yes, of a sort. It wasn't against any particular religion, it was against an overt display of any religious preference. In many jobs, this would not be a problem.

However, I was dealing with an international clientele, people are of all different religions. Some might be offended by particular religious displays. I'm not in agreement, or saying it is correct, it is just a fact of life.

If you are interested in doing global business, it is a fact that has to be considered. Also, if a company is hiring people to travel abroad, then some overt religious symbols might put them in danger.

When applying for a job that demands skill that will get you dirty, then many of my no-nos don't apply, such as clean fingernails if you want to be a garage mechanic. However, when I take my Toyota for service at my local dealership, the service manager who takes my information is always clean, nice nails and hands, neatly dressed in slacks and shirt with company logo on both shirt and jacket if it's cold.

In the San Francisco area, many companies are relaxed in their employees attire. If you are sure of that, you can dress accordingly. But still be neat, clean. Showing respect for a future employer is always key.

If you are looking for a job as a tattoo artist or to work in one of the tattoo parlors, then you can be a walking billboard and they probably won't mind. However, a bank in a retirement area might well be put-off.

> *Dress smart —look the part!*

The key is to use your common sense. Scope out a place if you can. Walk casually by at lunch or closing time and see what employees look like. What they are wearing?

Do you look like them? If you do, that will be the first thing HR will think about when you walk in the door. "They look like they work here." Always a good sign. Dress smart and look the part.

Let's talk about Facebook. This has become the pre-eminent tool for recruiters and human resources departments.

You can come in the door looking just fine and have a great interview. Chances are you will be told, "I'll get back to you." That gives HR time to check your references...and go on Facebook. Maybe also Linkedin. Twitter.

It would not be a good idea to get in your car and tweet something like, "just had interview w/hot babe in HR" or maybe 'old bag' or even 'bitch witch.' How about instead being smart and saying "interviewed w/fab company hope they like me" or something similar.

It would not be a good thing to have your Facebook page filled with pictures of you drinking, smoking pot, stoned, drunk, partying, fighting, showing more skin than you might in polite company, sexual comments, profanity, or sex acts. A good test is to not have anything you don't want your grandmother to see.

Let's also talk about individualism. If you are applying for a creative position, then it's probably a good thing. When I worked at Marvel Comics the writers and artists came in dressed how they wanted. We business people came in business clothes. We all looked like what we were. Think about dressing for a part in a play or a film. It can work wonders.

If you are applying for a position as a professional or business person, then work hard at looking like one. Go for the business look and once you are in the position see what the rest of the career professionals are wearing.

Chapter 5: The First Interview

Okay, you got in the door, now what? This is the big chance and it needs to be taken seriously, no matter what job you are applying for, a burger flipper or a top executive, the rules are the same.

Keep this in mind at all times: the company doesn't care about what it can do for you; it cares about what you can do for it. And that means, not only the company as a huge entity, but the person who will be your immediate superior. If you can make them look good, you are a good candidate, if you are a trouble maker, they look bad, hence a bad candidate.

In the current job market, recent graduates

are now competing with seasoned employees who have come into the job market because their companies have downsized or gone bankrupt.

They are older, more mature candidates with families, mortgages, college tuitions and vastly larger overheads to support than a recent graduate. They are also desperate and will take jobs well below their skill set just to put food on the family table. They understand business rules, are willing to work hard, go the extra mile, be on time, work overtime, and leave the attitude behind.

This is who you are competing with as well as the other graduates. It's not pretty out there and you have to develop and fine tune the tools to compete.

To start off on the right foot, check your attitude at home and think like a candidate, not someone who is entitled to the best job in the world. You are just one more candidate looking for a job, and with no experience, you have to WOW them!

Most companies are looking for team players

so if you think of yourself as an individualist, you might have to change your mind-set. They won't look at you as being interesting or creative if you are trying to present yourself as an individualist. Instead they might just see you as an oddball who probably won't fit in. However, if you are going for companies who hire geeks, fashion or creative, then you might get away with it – but remember you will still be up against older and smarter individualists with credentials and who probably know how to play the game better than you do, so be prepared to outshine them.

Go get a haircut, shave off all extraneous hair if you're a guy. If you want to keep the beard or moustache, make sure it's neatly trimmed. Guys, find a nail brush and use it, clean fingernails are a first turn off unless you are applying for a job as a mechanic.

For the women, get a manicure with a soft color and not-too-long nails. Have your hair neatly styled, not in your face or some odd style or color.

Remove all visible piercings, ear gages and cover all tattoos possible. You are trying to look professional and don't want to display that 'tramp stamp.'

Clothes should be neat, clean, pressed and professional looking. That means no odd styles or bizarre fashion statements other than jobs in the fashion industry. Ladies – no cleavage, no bare midriff, no very short skirts or spike heels – companies other than porno studios or Hooters generally don't want distractions in the workplace.

You can be fashionable, but not overtly sexual for most offices. If you don't know what to wear, go to your local bank and see what the female bank officers are wearing. It will generally be a simple dress, below the knee, sensible heel shoes, or a dark colored suit or skirt with a plain blouse; not too much jewelry or too much hair.

Gentlemen, I know you think "casual" is the thing, but it is a sign of respect for both the company and the interviewer, as well as yourself, to arrive looking as professional as possible with a tie, jacket, dress shirt and shined shoes. Yes - *shined shoes* – that means NO ATHLETIC SHOES, SANDALS OR SNEAKERS! No matter how much they cost. That is, unless job requires them.

> *...it is a sign of respect for both the company and the interviewer, as well as yourself, to arrive looking as professional as possible!*

When I hired men out of college to work for me, I suggested they have a wardrobe for international travel, world conventions and general business meetings that consisted of a navy or dark gray suit, a navy or black blazer and two pair of slacks – one gray and one beige. Dress shirts in white, light blue and yellow and conservative striped or paisley ties to match. Shoes might be loafer style to wear with the blazer and dress shoes to wear with the suit – both polished and clean. Any of the above combinations are acceptable for interviews.

If this is beyond your budget, go to the fanciest local thrift store and buy the best fitting second-hand clothes you can find until you are earning enough money to buy new.

You will be surprised what you can find in the local charity thrift stores and with a little dry cleaning and pressing, maybe a hem or two, you can look like royalty at your first interview...think "rock star of the business world!"

Remember that you were going to research the companies you were interested in? Now is the time to review all that research again and read every new press release you can find on the company you are going to interview with. That includes annual reports, financial statements, new management, anything you can find on the Internet.

This will give you discussion materials and the ability to speak about the company with some knowledge, or at the very least, ask intelligent questions. Just make sure to stay away from any detrimental gossip you may have found.

Chapter 6: 6 Secrets For A

Successful Interview

What every interviewer looks for and will
never tell you -

1. How you look – hair neat, clean
    hands and nails, shined shoes,
    clothing clean, pressed, matched
    and professional looking for the job
    being interviewed for. This is the
    first impression. It is the key to
    learn about how much you respect

yourself, the prospective job, the interviewer and the company.

2. Sit up straight, no slouch, make eye contact, don't fiddle with hands, fingers or pick nails. Don't sit with legs apart or put leg over your knee, keep knees together, no foot bouncing or fidgeting

3. Don't over talk interviewer; be concise, polite, and earnest.

4. Be careful of your body language - do lean forward a bit (this means you're interested), don't lean back and cross your arms over chest (means you think interviewer is full of bull and you've turned off)

5. Indicate you like to be helpful and are a team player.

6. If asked what your strongest points are use a positive response such as:

a. "I have a positive attitude about getting a job done correctly."

b. "I like to work and am eager to learn."

c. "I enjoy helping out others when I've completed my tasks."

d. "I don't like to stop working until the job is done.

e. Any positive attributes that best describe your personality.

Chapter 7: Interview Mistakes

I. Attitude: If you show you think you
know it all, or are so smart you
are "entitled" to a position, or
that a company is "lucky" to be
able to hire you— they won't.

II. Not ready for success:
Unshaven, bad grooming or
hygiene, hair ratty, bad posture,
all say you have no respect for
the company, the interviewer,
the job or yourself. Take two
steps back and go flip burgers
for the rest of your life.

III.   Over-selling or talking too much. Let the interviewer talk, make your responses short. It is okay to ask a few questions about the company and the position you are interviewing for. Being too gregarious is a great way to talk yourself out of a job and being branded as a "motor-mouth" or someone who just never shuts up.

IV.   Don't make faces; keep your expressions pleasant and bland. Think of keeping a poker face at all times except for smiles, they are always good.

V.   Don't bring anyone to the interview with you. A few years ago, parents went to interviews with candidates to make sure the company would be a "good fit for their brilliant graduate."

Forget it! Tell mom and dad to stay home. This is a sure way to be shown the door since you will be competing against mature candidates who don't need to bring mommy and daddy with them.

> *Attitude: If you think you know it all, or are so smart you are "entitled" to a position, or that a company is "lucky" to be able to hire you, chances are— they won't.*

Chapter 8: How To Move Up

I. Make your boss/supervisor look good

II. Do assigned tasks and a little bit more
   a. Anticipate needs
   b. Make the extra effort

III. Be on time for work or early – ***always!***

IV. Have all assignments, tasks ready, done on time and done correctly – ***always!***

V. Make your boss/supervisor look good

VI.   Excuses are never acceptable
        unless life threatening to you or
        family or an act of God beyond
        your control

VII. Make your boss/supervisor look
        good

VIII. Attitude at all times helpful,
        pleasant, open and respectful

IX.   Make your boss/supervisor look
        good

X.   Make the company look good.

XI.   Following the above rules makes
        you look good!

And yes, I did repeat the same phrase
several times. Good, you were paying
attention. Did you get the message? I hope
so.

Chapter 9: You're Fired!

It is difficult to get a job, but very easy to lose it. All you need is to think you can offer the same excuses you gave your parents, but at work, they don't have to accept them.

The main idea of work is to exchange your service for a company's money. Simple. You are being paid to perform a service, if you don't perform the service there is no reason to pay you.

If you *often* don't perform to expectations for the position, you will be fired. An employee that has to be told several times to do something is worthless. Your mother can ask you to take out the garbage five times and you can reply "later mom, I'm doing something." She might put up with it. She might swat you on the back of the head. She can't fire you, but she can throw you out of the house. Then you will really need a job to pay rent.

There is no, "I'll do it later" at work. If you are finishing up a previous task or doing work for someone in a higher position a more professional response is something like: "I'm also finishing up XYZ for Mr. or Ms Jones. How would you like me to prioritize these?"

Working for a company is working as part of a team. If you don't hold your end up, you will be let go.

Generally companies have policies about job reviews and warnings before being let go. Take them to heart, read them since you can be fired with cause. This is very serious. On your next resume you will have to list the companies where you last worked, and if HR checks, they will find out you were fired with cause.

If the company is omitted from your resume, there will be a time lapse you will be asked to account for. There are many acceptable time lapses such as pregnancy, company layoffs or cutbacks, and bankruptcies. With so many available candidates, HR is tasked with carefully checking resumes and making sure that all work references are included.

Think of Donald Trump looking at you and saying those words you never want to hear - "You're fired!"
These are some of **the thirty ways** it can happen.

I.   Late to work or miss work too often with unacceptable excuses

II.   Sloppy work product

III.   Unacceptable appearance

IV.   Work assignments not done in a timely manner

V.   Work handed in incorrectly

VI.   Sloughing off work on other team members

VII.   Gossiping about company, boss or other employees

VIII.   Back stabbing boss, supervisor or others

IX.   Sullen or bad attitude

X.   Not complying with requests

XI.   Using "I forgot" as excuse – this
        means you weren't interested
        enough to remember

XII.   Challenging supervisor or boss

XIII.   Excessive arguing

XIV.   Playing computer games at work

XV.   Too many personal phone calls

XVI.   Texting during work hours

XVII.   Not available at work station
        when needed

XVIII. Taking too long for breaks

XIX.   Rude or disrespectful behavior to
        supervisor or others

XX.   Improper sexual behaviors-
        flirting, touching, insinuating

XXI.   Improper clothing-revealing,
        unkempt, unsightly

XXII.   Employee romance against
        company policy

XXIII. Leaking trade secrets

XXIV. Failure to disclose criminal record

XXV. Illegal immigration status

XXVI. Nasty comments about company, boss or co-workers on Facebook

XXVII. Excessive profanity

> *...those words you never want to hear – "You're fired!*

XXVIII. Fighting or aggressive behavior towards co-workers

XXIX. Striking another employee

XXX. Making rude or nasty comments on Facebook about boss, co-workers or company

And many more ways...

Large companies have printed policy handbooks available at Human Resources and you can ask for one.

Get informed about company policies to make sure you don't hear the Donald's words.

Chapter 10: Don't Jump Ship

No one ever said it was going to be easy, but if you keep at it and don't give up, you will eventually find a job.

The key is to remember that whoever is doing the hiring is doing so to make the company successful, not you. If you can hold that image in your mind during interviews, and have done your research into the company and its direction and financial status, it should assist you to direct your responses in a way that will make you stand out at as a candidate.

Keep in mind that finding a job is a job!

So let's review the steps you are going to take to make this job search a success:

1. Start with your lists:
    a. skills, hobbies, interests
    b. where you would like to live
    c. cost of living, include moving if
necessary

2. Find companies that interest you in order
of preference
    d. research companies for openings,
financial situation, location

3.   Prepare your resume and yourself
    e. prepare yourself for the work of finding
a job
    f. target where you want to start applying
and do your research
    g. check your appearance and clothes:
dress smart—look the part

4. The first interview, review your research
on the company and how you can benefit it
    h. during the interview, be alert, polite and
show interest and knowledge of the
company. This is the time to ask some
intelligent questions about its future direction.
    i. this is the time to pitch yourself, your
work ethic and willingness to get
the job done and on time

j. don't over-talk interviewer or talk too much

5. Once you have the job make sure you are the model employee
    k. on time, ready to go, limit personal phone, texting, computer use
    l. stay clear of office politics
    m. no mention of job on Facebook other than in good light

You are well on your way to getting and keeping one of the best jobs.

Chapter 11: ...and for good

measure - Alice's Golden Rules:

Here are two golden rules that are often ignored and can set you back for months, often times—years.

Never quit a job until you have your next job in place.

It is always easier to find a job when you are working, you have references and inherent in your working status is that some company found you worthwhile enough to hire.

If you are unemployed after working, either you've been fired for not being up to snuff, you quit which a future employer might take as being difficult to work with and not into working for the long haul, or perhaps you've been laid off as a company has down-sized. The last option is not a negative in the current marketplace and is easily overcome. The other two, not so much.

So don't quit. Keep your eyes and ears open for other positions in your industry, make friends in other companies, and network quietly. Do not let the information that you are looking for another position get around where you are currently working. Often you might miss an opportunity for advancement within the same company if they think you are a dissatisfied employee.

If you must quit, make sure you have enough money stashed away to live for a year on unemployment. Yes, I said a year. Think how long it took you to find the job you are quitting from. Look at the unemployment statistics. Don't quit without your next job. Trust me on this.

<u>Never</u> Threaten To Quit Unless You Advance Or Get A Raise

I have seen this ploy backfire too many times to mention. The general response from management is simple: "We'll be sorry to see you go, but please pack up your things, security will show you out." And just like that, you are on the street or in the parking lot with your coffee mug and plant in a transfile box and have to start the whole job process all over again.

If you think you should have a raise or want to ask for a better position, make a reasonable case for yourself. Talk about extra work and responsibilities you have assumed.

Tell supervisor about classes you have taken to improve your work or your skill set.

You might politely say you have gotten married and are expecting a new addition since you have been working for the company and this has added to your expenses.

And then there are the No-Nos:

Do Not do the following:
Ask when you can expect a raise when you are interviewing.

Ask for a raise when you have worked for the company less than a year unless at the time of hiring a review was promised sooner.

Say that you heard so and so got a raise and you should too.

Say that you want to have more money because you need it. You knew what the job paid when you took it, that means you didn't know how to budget.

Do not say you need money to buy something like a television or a new tablet.

Or, even worse, don't say that you know people at a competing company are making more money. That opens the door to a response like, "You can always go and work there."

If you get turned down, wait about six months and try again, with logical reasons about how you are benefiting the company, how your skills have improved so you are worth more than when you were hired, and the positive things you have done to either bring in more money, or save the company money. Remember, your worth as an employee is measured in dollars and cents.

Good luck! I wish you happy hunting and hope you find the perfect job to suit your talents. There is seldom a better life than one in which you get up each morning with a smile because you are looking forward to another day at work at a place that gives you pleasure and a career that fulfills you. An average working life spans many years, so consider where you will enjoy spending them.

Alice Donenfeld

www.ingramcontent.com/pod-product-compliance
Lightning Source LLC
Chambersburg PA
CBHW050547210326
41520CB00012B/2752